Stories of the Road Allowance People

Translated and Put on Paper by
Maria Campbell

Paintings by
Sherry Farrell Racette

Library and Archives Canada Cataloguing in Publication

Stories of the road allowance people / translated by Maria Campbell ; paintings by Sherry Farrell Racette. -- Rev. ed.

ISBN 978-0-920915-99-8

1. Métis--Folklore. 2. Oral tradition--Prairie Provinces. I. Campbell, Maria

II. Gabriel Dumont Institute of Native Studies and Applied Research

E99.M47S76 2010   398.2089'970712   C2010-905478-4

Gabriel Dumont Institute Project Team:

Darren R. Préfontaine, Project Leader and Editor
David Morin, Graphic Designer
Karon Shmon, Director, Publishing
Globe Printers, Saskatoon, Printer

The Gabriel Dumont Institute acknowledges the financial support of the Office of the Federal Interlocutor for Métis and Non-Status Indians, Indian and Northern Affairs Canada for the production and publishing of this resource.

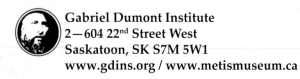

Canada

Gabriel Dumont Institute
2—604 22nd Street West
Saskatoon, SK S7M 5W1
www.gdins.org / www.metismuseum.ca

DEDICATED TO
THOMAS (TJ),
MICHEL, MOSES,
ALEXANDER, JULIEN,
SHANNON, AND LIAM

CONTENTS

INTRODUCTIONS, 2

FOREWORD BY RON MARKEN, 6

DAH RED-HEADED FUR BUYER, 8

GOOD DOG BOB, 18

DAH SONG OF DAH CROW, 24

ROU GAROUS, 34

LA BEAU SHA SHOO, 51

BIG JOHN, 64

JACOB, 79

JOSEPH'S JUSTICE, 92

DAH TEEF, 108

AFTERWORD BY PAUL DEPASQUALE, 122

INTRODUCTIONS

PUBLISHER'S INTRODUCTION

The Gabriel Dumont Institute (GDI) is very pleased to publish Maria Campbell's *Stories of the Road Allowance People: The Revised Edition*. It is an honour for the Institute to publish this book. A highly-acclaimed and award-winning writer, playwright, filmmaker, Elder, and activist, Maria has been an inspiration, role model, and mentor for countless Métis.

First published in 1995, *Stories of the Road Allowance People* has become a staple of Native Studies, History, and English classes in campuses across Canada, and remains the finest collection of traditional Métis stories available. Out-of-print for several years, countless community people have asked for it to be reprinted. As a result, both Maria and GDI decided to publish this revised edition which includes the new story, "Dah Red-Headed Fur Buyer," a narration component, and new art by Sherry Farrell Racette.

Stories of the Road Allowance People is an enduring resource because it remains true to the original voice of the Michif Elders who originally told Maria these stories. Written in distinct Michif accents or "Village English," these stories hearken back to a time when the Oral Tradition was the main means to relate cultural knowledge. While the Métis have an age-old storytelling tradition which seamlessly blends Cree, Ojibway, French-Canadian, and Scots stories and motifs, very little has been done to chronicle traditional their stories. This anthology provides an authentic attempt to recreate this vibrant storytelling tradition by focusing on more recent, historically-based oral stories rather than the creation narratives found in Wiisakaychak, Nanabush, and Chi-Jean stories.

These retellings are very poignant, and the emotions that emerge from them are visceral and engaging. For instance, as readers and listeners we laugh at the spectacle of someone sharing a jug of wine at the Pearly Gates with the Son of God. We also find humour in the rich Métis nicknaming tradition which finds its way into the book with such colourful nicknames as "Josephine Jug of Wine." At the other end of the emotional spectrum, we feel empathy for the lonely elderly couple who can't express the depth of their feelings for one another because of social constraints. We feel empathy as well for the socially-ostracized woman who was transformed into a rou garou for not embracing Catholicism. We also feel indignant at the resigned sense of injustice felt by the storytellers for the racist, colonizing regime imposed on First Nations and Métis people. Readers and listeners are therefore clearly engaged in the emotive qualities of these stories, and while they seem at first glace innocuous and entertaining, they clearly serve a purpose, and possess a myriad of meanings, depending on who is reading or listening to them. As a result, they are as complex as any form of written literature. Once you've read *Stories of the Road Allowance People* or better yet have someone read it to you, you'll never forget these stories, and perhaps more importantly, you'll have a keener understanding of the Métis worldview. For this reason alone, this book remains one of the most priceless examples of Métis literature.

Maarsi,

GDI Publishing Department
Saskatoon, Saskatchewan
August 2010

INTRODUCTION

I remember a warm kitchen on a stormy winter night. I am sitting on the floor with my Cheechum and the old ladies. The room is full of grandpas, mammas and papas, aunties, uncles, and cousins. There is laughter, hot sweet tea, and the smell of red willow tobacco. "Hahawew kiyas mana kisayanoo kee achimoot ... Long ago the old man told us this story," my uncle would begin, and my Cheechum and the old ladies would puff their pipes and nod. "Tapew anima, tapew ... Yes, yes it is true."

This was the first snowfall and the first night of storytelling in the little road allowance village where I grew up. If someone knocked on our door, my papa would call out, "Tawow, pay peetiqwak ... Come in, there is room." My mamma would pour another cup of hot tea, and people would make room for the visitor, who would lean forward and become a part of our circle.

Today, the stories I heard then, I have learned, and I have been given permission to share them with you. They are old men's stories. I had hoped when I became a student of storytelling that I would get old women teachers, but that was not meant to be. The old women were kind, made me pots of tea, cooked me soup and bannock, made me starblankets and moccasins, then sent me off to the old men who became my teachers.

I am a very inexperienced storyteller compared to the people who taught me. And although I speak my language, I have had to relearn it, to decolonize it, or at least begin the process of decolonization. This has not been an easy task, and the journey has taken me many years. I have paid for the stories by relearning and rethinking my language, and by being a helper or servant to the teachers. I have also paid for the stories with gifts of blankets, tobacco, and even a prize Arab stallion.

With the stories, I have had lifetimes of "stuff" put into my memory. I am not even sure what it all is, but the teachers say, "Don't worry about it, just think that your brain is the computer you use, and we are the people typing it in. When you need it, or you have had the experience to understand it, your spirit will give it to you." I have learned to trust them. It is in this spirit that I share these stories with you. I give them to you in the dialect and rhythm of my village, and my father's generation. I am responsible for all the mistakes.

Today, fifteen years later, I am still responsible for all the mistakes, and I am even more grateful for the journey I began with these old men and the "stuff" they put into my memory. Over the past fifteen years people have asked me many questions about these stories but most frequently, the question has been, "Who are the Road Allowance People?"

You will have to do your own research on that history as space does not permit me that today. However, I can tell you that the name Road Allowance People was coined by white government officials and land owners to describe the dispossessed Métis people who, having no where to go after the Resistance of 1885, built their homes on unoccupied crown lands, more often land that had been set aside for highways or roads. As these crown lands were developed and roads were built, the people were chased out, their homes burned, and in many cases their children scooped up by child welfare agencies. The last community to be dispersed in Saskatchewan was Crescent Lake just outside of Yorkton in 1962. You may contact the Gabriel Dumont Institute for more information or the Métis National Council.

I would like to take this opportunity to thank you for the many requests to republish this book. I hope you enjoy the new story. It is about a special storyteller, and it is also about John Diefenbaker, who was well liked by our people because he made for great storytelling.

I acknowledge and honour my teachers who have now all passed on: my father, John (Dan) Campbell, Peter O-Chiese, Leonard Pamburn, and Dolphus Roulette. My great-uncles, Gabriel and William Vandal, my uncle Alex Vandal, Adrian Hope, and Mederic McDougall. Still living is Maruis Iron who is now 93-years-old, and is still my teacher, my good friend, and now my adopted father. I thank him for his continuing kindness and generosity, and I thank his family for sharing him with me.

I dedicate these stories to the descendants of Road Allowance People everywhere, to their strength and resilience, and for the good work they do that keeps us together as a people and a nation. Stories always suffer in translation and it is difficult sometimes to put into English the richness of a people's life and culture. The diversities, the unique identities, characteristics, territories, and histories become obscure or forgotten in the struggle to survive, but I have learned that they are always rediscovered when working with Elders. As Metis people, we have so much to celebrate, and our diversity is one of them, the other is our sense of humour.

I offer a special thank you to the following people, Sherry Farrell Racette who loved the stories and gave them life through her art. Billyjo DeLaRonde and Roy Poitras for giving them voice, Gilbert Anderson and John Arcand for their good music. Ron Marken and Paul DePasquale for their kind words and friendship. Marci, Gabriel Dumont Institute for being here for us. Karon Shmon, Darren Prefontaine, and David Morin for making it possible to republish this book, for its editing and layout and most of all, your kindness through a very difficult time. Thank you also to Wayne Giesbrecht of Media Access & Production, University of Saskatchewan. Thank you to the University of Alberta and the Whitehorse Public Library, for making it possible for me to do these translations, Jeanette Armstrong and Theytus Books for publishing the first edition. I thank my siblings, my lodge family, and my close friends for always being there. To my children—Roxanne, Tanice, Daniel, Cynthia, and Gregory, who traveled the miles with me and to Leslie, the new addition to my family, and to my son in-laws, my beautiful grandchildren, and great grandchildren. I love you all and I am blessed to have you in my life.

Maria Campbell
Gabriel's Crossing
September 12, 2010

 FOREWORD

"We Still Believe What We Hear"

Irish poet Seamus Heaney, in a poem for his mother, an unschooled woman, describes how she conversed with her son, the famous poet: "With more challenge than pride, she'd tell me, 'You know them things.'" How does the famous poet respond to her loving modesty? "So I governed my tongue/In front of her." What Maria Campbell has brought to this book is a loving and painstaking governing of tongues, oral tradition printed on white pages, words to get your ears around. And she has done it with the careful respect of a child for a parent. Like the Irish writers she loves so much, Maria sustains her written/oral narratives with honour for minor eccentricities of belief and behaviour, celebrating the triumphs and joys of our common humanity. The result: "We still believe what we hear," as Heaney says in his poem *The Singer's House.*

The accents and grammar of the narratives you will hear in this book are uncommon, but do not make the mistake of thinking they lack sophistication. Their rhythms and vocabulary are not those of the school textbooks. Instead, they coil and spin lightly around the lives and voices of a complex and courageous people. Standard English cannot appropriately or fully accommodate the voices Maria Campbell assembles here; the authority and music will not be denied:

> Dere wasen very much he can steal from dah table anyways
> cept dah knifes and forks
> An Margareet he knowed he wouldn dare take dem
> cause dat woman you know
> hees gots a hell of a repetation for being a hardheaded woman
> when he gets mad.
> Dat man he have to be a damn fool to steal from hees table.
> (*Dah Teef*)

Reading the speeches in John M. Synge's Irish plays, you will not be immersed in "standard" English either yet the colour and power of his words are immense:

> Its queer joys they have, and who knows the thing they'd do, if it'd make
> the green stones cry itself to think of you swaying and swiggling at the butt
> of a rope, and you with a fine, stout neck, God bless you! The way you'd
> be half an hour; in great anguish, getting your death. (*The Playboy of the Western World*)

Finally, we must do more than simply read this book. Book culture is eye culture. Most of us imagine through our eyes. Of course, we should feast on these stories with our eyes, and the book gives us a bountiful feast in Sherry Farell Racette's fantastic illustrations. But it is essential that we read the stories with ours ears first. Say them aloud. Listen to them with our friends. Light a fire and speak them to the children and grandchildren. These stories and poems have come a long journey to be with us, from Michif through literal translations through the Queen's Imperial English, and back to the earth in village English. Listen to their tales. The main reason for their tortuous route is Maria's need to have us hear the voices—breathing, laughing, sighing human voices.

Our European concepts of "voice" are hedged with assumptions and undermined with problems. Voice equals speech. Voice commands the floor. Voice is authority. To have voice is to have power. To speak is to hold others in sway, to register opinion. To be dumb or voiceless is synonymous with being ignorant. Even the distinguished notion of "oral tradition" has been charged with bad odours by our professors and critics: "Poetry belonging to this tradition is composed orally. ... As a rule it is the product of illiterate or semi-literate societies" (O.A. Cuddon, *The Penguin Dictionary of Literary Terms and Literary Theory*, pg. 659). Statements like Cuddon's, as a rule, are the product of arrogant and heedless societies. Degrade or silence the voices, and you kill the cultures. Take away a people's language, insult its ways of expression, and you rub out their singularity and character.

That's why this is an important book. It is one more record in the long undertaking that turns up the volume of the oral tradition, a tradition that goes deeper than Moses. These are the voices of storytellers and of a culture. They have nothing to do with being illiterate; they have everything to do with assertion and eloquence—self-governing of the tongue can lead to all sorts of self-government.

Ron Marken, Saskatoon
September 2010

DAH RED-HEADED FUR BUYER

In dah ole days you know

we had nutting but trouble wit dem fur buyers.

Oh dah odd one he was okey

but most of dem dey was very bad.

Well I suppose dey have to make a living too

but dey don have to cheat us like dey do.

Dey was real bad.

One time we had a red-headed woman come to our country to buy fur.

Oh he was a hell of a looker.

But he was a bigger cheat den all dah res of dem.

An us

we can do nutting

cause we was gentlemans an he was a lady.

During dis time too

we gots dis guy living wit us.

He come from down sout someplace when he was a young man

an he marry up wit one of our womans an dey raise a family.

He never done much work dat man

jus kine of lay aroun all day an go visiting at night.

But he was a hell of a storyteller an a good singer too

so dah peoples dey look after him an hees family.

Dey make shore dey got lots of meat

an hees wife an kids dey always make a big garden so dey live okey.

No better no worse den dah res of us.

By dah way

dey call dis man Frankeesis cause he was kinda small.

In dis story

him an hees family dey come wit us

when we go picking berries an digging sinkah roots

in dah nashanal park.

Lots of us road allowance peoples use to do dat to earn a living in dem days.

Every summer dere would be lots of us out picking and digging.

Sometimes 15 or 20 families

an we all travel wit wagons an horses an we live in tents.

He was real hard work but we do it anyways.

Well of course we gots to or we'll go hungry.

But he was a good life an he was clean.

An all of us peoples we stay close togedder

not like today

when dah relations dey never see each udder.

Anyways we pick an dig all summer.

An when we fill up all dah bags wit roots and everyting else wit berries

we load up an we go to Prince Albert to sell dem.

We use sell our berries an roots in dat town an we did pretty good too.

Never gets rich you know but we make a few good dollars

an everybody he have a good visit wit dere relatives.

We use to set up our camp across dah river in dah jack pines
not too far from dah nuisance grouns.
We camp dere sometimes for a week
selling our roots an berries in dah town
an visiting wit our relatives on dah Fox Farm.
Dat was a road allowance village not far from our camp an some of us
we was related to dah peoples dere.

We always like camping in dat place
cause dah nuisance grouns he was a very good one.
Dem whites peoples you know dey trowed away real good stuff
an us we could shore use it.
All we gots to do is jus wash it an fix it up.
Yes sir you could dress like a real big shot you know
an really fix up your wagon real good jus from dat place.

Well dis one day we was just starting to pack up to go home
when dah kids dey come running.
"Hurry up," dey yell. "Come an see what Frankeesis hees doing."
We all run as fas as we can
cause if Frankeesis hees doing something
den hees gonna be a good story
cause dat man he don do nutting unless hees making a story.

Well dere he was him an hees wife
dey was pounding a bunch of willows around dat nuisance groun.
Dey have a big hole at one end and dey was building a fence around it.
A real big one.

We all watch for a long time

tryin to figure out what dey was doing

den our ole uncle Pahchuneese he start to laugh.

"Well sun of a gun." He says.

"Dat Frankeesis hees building an ole time buffalo jump."

An shore enough dats what he was doing.

When he see us watching him

he start walking aroun checking it good

den he he tell us.

"Youse are all invited to a feas on Monday.

Me an my family we're gonna have a big party

so bring all dah gitars an fiddles."

Den he signal hees kids

an dey pick up ole pots an pans

an dey start banging dem an yelling an making a hell of a racket.

Well purdy soon

a whole bunch of house rats dey come running.

Dem rats dey look like a black river

an dey run right into dat hole an

Frankeesis an hees wife dey start shooting dem.

An us peoples we watch dem

an we try an figure out what hees gonna do wit dem rats.

But we never ask him

cause dats hees story an we jus gots to wait.

Well we go back to our camp
laughing an talking
bout what dat man hees gonna do.
He shore cause lots of excitement an talk dats for shore.
A couple of days later
me an Alec we was getting ready to ride to dah town when
Frankeesis he come over an he say,
"When you get to town Danny
can you send dat fur buyer here an tell him I gots fur to sell."

Hoo boy

dah whole camp he was almos crazy

when we tell dem what hees gonna do

an dey all wait for dat red-headed fur buyer to come.

Well he come alright

an he was looking real good on hees tunder black horse

an he buy all dem rats an he cheat Frankeesis real bad.

At leas he tink he cheat him.

Dat night Frankeesis an hees woman an kids

dey have a hell of a feas for dah camp.

We had buloney, garlic sausage and macaronee.

White bread an can tumatoes.

Dere was apples for dah kids

an lumnash for dah ole peoples.

Chockluts for dah womans an wine for us mans

an boy

we sing an dance all night an have a hell of a good time.

Wherever we go all dat summer

an after we get home

we tell dah story over an over again an we laugh like hell.

Den one day dah Mounties dey come.

Dey ask for Frankeesis an we follow dem to hees house.

Everybody he was standing outside

when dey bring him out.

"I'll see you later boys." He says

an dey put him in dah car an drive away.

Well us mans we all go to Prince Albert

an we hire John Diefenbaker to be hees lawyer

an we all go to dah court.

When dah court he start dah policemans dey bring Frankeesis in

an he smile an wave at us.

Diefenbaker him

he come in all dress up an he look real good.

You know perfeshnal.

He was a very smart man dat Diefenbaker

he become dah Prime Minister of dis whole country you know.

An he was a good one too.

He give us Indians an Halfbreeds canned buloney.

Spork I tink hees call.

I don care too much for it myself but at leas he give us someting.

Dats more den anyone else he do in dem days.

Well anyways dat John Diefenbaker he win dat case.

He win it on a tec ni cal itee dey call it.

Diefenbaker he tell dat judge

"He sell him rats your honour. He did not sell dat woman muskrats.

Here are hees witnesses."

An he point at all of us an we nod.

Dats true you know he sell dat red-headed fur buyer rats.

Hees not hees fault if dat woman he tought dey was muskrats.

Boy dat Frankeesis he come home a big hero.

Dah womans dey have a party for him an dey sen dah boys out on horseback

to invite people from all over to come

cause hees not often we win two times us people.

Dat Frankeesis not only beat dah fur buyer but he beat dah court too.

We invite John Diefenbaker to come to dah party too

but he was too busy helping udder pour peoples.

An dat red-headed fur buyer

well him he leave dah country an no one he ever heered bout him again.

Too bad he have to cheat cause hes was a real looker.

We gets a new fur buyer

a good one for a change.

Dis one hees an ole man an he knowed hees furs

an he give us a fair price.

An dat Frankeesis

he live to be an ole man an he make lots of stories.

But he never make anudder one one as good as dah one bout

dah red-headed fur buyer.

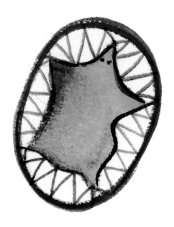

 Good Dog Bob

I shore do lots of stupid tings when I was a boy.

Real stupid tings.

Sometime I learn a lesson from what I do

sometime I don know what I learn.

I work as a freighter one winter when I was bout fourteen.

My Mudder he let me use our horses

so I join up wit a freighting company at Big River.

We was forty teams an we haul way up nort.

It use to take one mont

from dah time we leave Big River til we get dere.

An it use to get forty below

sometime even colder

but we still gots to work.

I use to get so cold an lonesome but I gots to act

like a man cause I got my own team.

One time we stop at a small settlement for dah night.

Dere was only womans an kids

cause dah mans dey was all out on dah traplines.

Well dis one woman

he keep on coming aroun our camp

an he keep on making signs for me to follow him.

Dah mans dey tease

an tell me to go wit him.

I guess dey taught I been wit a woman before.

Well me
I don wan dem to know I was stupid
so I go wit dis woman to hees shack.
Hees man was gone trapping so he tole me not to worry
jus get in dah bed wit him.

I don know what to do me
cause I never done dis before but I was shore trying
when all of a sudden
someone he bang on dah door an dat woman he sit up
an he say
"Holy Mary Mudder of God! Dats my ole man.
He come home early."

Hoo boy!
I was so scare I don know what to do
I can even tink.
It seem like my brains he quit working.
"Go under dah bed! Misi mase tah tayo awasis." Dah
woman he say
"Stay dere until my man he fall asleep. Den you get
out fas!"

Well dat man he was glad to be home
an he start right away to boder hees woman.
When dey start dere business
dey bump me.
"What's dat?"
Dah man he ask hees woman.

"Oh dats your dog Bob" Dah woman he say.

"He always sleep under dere when your gone."

Dah man he put hees han on dah floor an he say

"Astum Bob."

Well me I gots to preten I was Bob

so I tap dah floor wit my han

you know

like a dog hees tail.

An den I pant an I lick hees han.

Boy dat shore makes him happy

"Good dog Bob" he say

an he go back to hees business.

Well finely dat man he fall asleep

soon as he start to snore hees woman he whisper

"Sip way tay."

He shore don gots to worry bout me cause I'm already halfway

to dah door.

When I get dah door open

I run like hell in my bare arse to dah camp.

I los my panses by dah shack

but I was to scare to go back an look for dem.

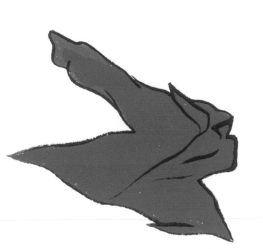

You know dat woman
he went an tole anudder woman an dat one
he tell hees husban.
An by dinner time
all dah mans dey heered what happen.
Boy did I ever get dah teasing.
"Good dog Bob" all dah mans dey say
an dey laugh like hell.

Boy I was shore stupid.
You know
dat man he could of kill me.
I gots no business in hees bed.
I bodder lots of womans in my life. But me I never
bodder no one else hees bed after dat.

Dah Song of Dah Crow

I'm gonna tell you bout dis man called Crow.

I meet him not too long ago.

I heerd lots bout him over dah years

but I never knowed him in person before.

Hees a good man

one of dem peoples dat belong in dah ole days

you know dah kine I mean.

Dere starting to come back again

tank dah God for dat.

Me I was scared we was turning white

but a few years ago

dah times dey start to change.

Dey say dat Crow

he was born somewhere in dah sudern country

but nobody he knowed for shore.

Jus hees Mudder I guess

But no one he knowed dat woman at all.

Me

I heerd he was raised by ole peoples

an dey teach him all kines of tings

bout dah ole days.

You know

dey even say dat man he can talk to dah eagles.

Dats true!

An me I believe on it

cause dah man dat tole me dat

he never tell lies.

Dey say dat Crow

he travel all over dah damn country when he growed up.

He travel by horse by dah car

an he even travel on dah foot.

Ooh he done lots of travelling dat man

an he meet a hell of a pile of peoples

an he live wit dem too.

Some of dem dey was black

udders dey was white.

He live wit dah cowboys too

an dey say

he even live dah wit yellow ones.

I guess dat was in dah States

cause him

he live dere too.

Dah peoples dat tell me bout him
dey say he was a good man.
Oh yeah
dat Crow he have good blood.
Good man you know
he come from good blood.
Dats right.
Dah ole peoples dey use to say dat.

Well dis Crow he was a wile one I guess.
Every damn place you go
you heered stories bout him.
You heered dem on dah reservation
in dah halfbreed country
an in dah towns an dah cities.
You even heered dem stories in dah jails.

Dah stories dere not bad you know
jus crazy.
Nobody knows for shore what hees true.
I don tink nobody he care eeder.
Dey jus tell dah stories
cause Crow
he makes damn good storytelling.

Some mans dere like dat you know
specially dem ones dat gots black eyes.
Me I don know what it ees bout dem
but dey make good stories.

Dah Crow hees a good man like I say before
but hees got lots of weakness
an one of dem he was gambling.
An anudder one
he was womans.
An dats what he always gets him into dah trouble.

One time I heered bout dis Blackfoot woman
he win him in a poker game.
Not dat Crow he plays wit womans like dat.
Oh no!
Dah womans dey gots lots of respec for him
cause he treat dem decent.

But dis Blackfoot woman
he gots a man
dat was real cruel wit him
beating him up an running aroun.
Ole Dumont you know
hees dah one dat tell me dis story.
An ole Dumont him
he comes from Montana
an he see it wit hees own eyes.

I guess dat woman hees man

he was slapping him aroun

so dah Crow he tell him

"If dat woman hees so bad,

you might as well bet him in dis game."

Ole Dumont he say,

if Crow he try taking dat woman any udder way

dat man he would of jus kill him.

But hees shore funny issn it?

Dat man he don know bout Crow.

Course maybe

hees jus been too damn busy giving hees woman a bad time

an he never heerd none of dah stories.

But anyways

he bet dah woman an he lost.

Well

I guess he wasen very happy.

But what can he do?

Dat night when Crow an dat woman dey was asleep

dah door he fly open

an dis gambler he come in.

Boy!

I guess he have a skinning knife in hees han

an he was madder den hell.

He jump dah Crow from behine
an he stick dat knife in hees back.
Ole Dumont he say
dah blood he was all over
an dey was shore Crow he was dead.

I guess dat Blackfoot woman he go crazy.
Cause dah Crow you know
he was dah firs man dat ever treat him good.

Dat woman
him too he grab a knife
an he cut dat gambler all up real good.
Damn well bout time too if you ask me.
Cause a man hees no good for nutting if he beat up hees woman.
Dat woman he should of done it a long time ago.

Well anyways
dat man he was scare
an he run like hell
an nobody he seed him ever since.
Dats a hell of a way issn it
to make a repetation for yourself.
Beating up womans
using dem to gamble
den having your woman put dah run on you.
Me I shore as hell would never show my face eeder.

Well you know

dah Crow he never die dat night

but he come damn close.

Ole Dumont he say

dat woman he heal him.

I guess dat woman he was an Indian doctor.

Deres lots of dem kine of womans

even today.

Dere good womans

dey jus got no account mans.

Well when dah Crow he gets all better

dat woman he leave him.

He love him alright

but whats dah use of staying?

He knowed dah Crow he can settle down.

Dat man he was always moving

an dats how I meet him.

He end up in our part of dah country.

Ooh like I tell you

we heered lots bout him before he end up over here

but we never seed him before.

Oh he was an one of us alright

no question bout dat.

Hees all dark wit lines on hees face

an hees got scars all over.

He wear cowboy boots

he buy dem in Texas I tink

an he wear a bull riding hat wit silver on it.

An hees a good lookin man

strong.

Dah kine you tell stories bout.

But you don wan to make him mad

not less you wan somebody to tell a story bout you.

Me

I kinda like him.

He look wile an high blooded.

Long time since I seed a man like dat.

"Ay tip aimsoot,"

dah ole people dey use to say bout a man like him.

He own hisself.

Well

dats was until a few weeks ago anyways.

Now me
I don know what hees gonna happen.
Cause dat man you know
he get mixed up wit a Halfbreed woman.
Dats right!
An you know dat woman
he talks to dah eagles too.

Rou Garous

You ever heered bout dah Rou Garous?

Never!

Me I taught everybody he knowed bout dem.

Well dere humans you know

jus like you an me

but someting he happen to dem an dey turn to dogs in dah night.

Dats right!

Some of dem dey even turn into wolfs.

Dats shore funny issn it?

How tings like dat dey can happen on dis eart.

Me I knowed our relations dah Indians

dah ole time ones dat is.

Dey could turn demselves into animals

even birds.

My ole Granfawder he could turn hisself into a bear.

An I knowed dis ole woman when I was a boy

dat one he turn hisself into a kiyute.

But dey do dat to doctor peoples dat was sick.

Dese Rou Garous

dey was different.

Dey was bad tings from dah dark side of dah eart

lees I tink dey was from dah dark side.

Maybe I tink dat cause dats what dah Prees he tell us.

He claims dere use to be lots of dem in dah ole days

dat was before all of us become good Catlics.

He say dat dah Rou Garou

he don like dah Jesus an dah Virgin Mary.

Oh no.

Dah Rou Garou he only like dah darkness an all dah

tings dat go wit it.

Well me I never seed one

an I shore never wan to eeder.

Long time ago I knowed dis ole man

hees name he was Harry T'staymow.

Dat means tobacco in our language but us

we call him Chi Kaw Chee.

He live wit a woman one time an dat woman he was a Rou Garou.

Josephine Jug of Wine dat woman he was called.

Dat not hees real name.

Dey call him dat cause he live in dah big city for a long time.

I member my Mudder he gets real mad when we call dat woman dat.

He say Josephine he don never drink hees whole life

an we got no respec for calling him dat.

My Mudder he never knowed dat woman but he have dah seeing

an always know bout tings like dat.

My Mudder he say

jus cause Josephine he don believe on dah Jesus an dah Virgin Mary

dat don give us dah right to call him a name like dat.

You know

my Mudder he always believe dat we was all getting crazy

from dis Catlic stuff.

I never tell many peoples dis

but my Mudder you know

he was never a Catlic.

Hee jus preten all hees life

an dat way

dah Prees he don know dat some of dah peoples dey was

fooling aroun wit dah ole way.

Anyways in dis story

I was out on dah trapline wit my Uncle Tommy

when we heered some wolfs howling.

I guess dats what makes him member.

He tell me

dat Chi Kaw Chee he meet Josephine in dah city when

he go to see dah army doctor.

Chi Kaw Chee he have a bad foot you know
dat foot he was bad from dah day he was borned
so he can join dah army.
He was damn lucky
cause darn near all dah mans from our part of dah country
dey go to dah war an dey gets kill.

Well my Uncle Tommy

he say dat Josephine he wasen like dah udder womans.

For one ting

he like to walk aroun in dah dark by hees ownself.

Dah womans aroun here

dey don do tings like dat.

Lees not unless dey have to.

Deres big hills in our part of dah country

an a big lake.

Well my Uncle Tommy he say dat woman

he walk all over dem ridges an all aroun dah lake.

An jus bout every night

dah peoples dey could hear a wolf howling.

Dats right!

An dere was no wolfs in our part of dah country in dem days.

Lees no one seed any for nearly fifty years.

My Uncle Tommy

he say dat Josephine he was a real good lookin woman.

Tall an well built.

An my Uncle he say dat woman

he have differen kine of eyes from dah res of dah peoples.

Josephine hees eyes dey was slanted an yellow

an dey was real wile.

You know

dah kine some animals dey gots.

You NEVER can tame dat kine of animal.

Wolfs dey gots dem kine of eyes

an kiyutes an lynxes.

You know dat woman

dey say he was like a lone wolf too

he never make no friens wit nobody.

Oh shore

he visit dah peoples

but he only do dat

when Chi Kaw Chee he go wit him.

But he never go alone.

He was one of dem peoples dat comes an goes

but nobody he know him.

Deres some peoples like dat on dis eart you know

course I don tink dere all Rou Garous.

Well some of dem maybe.

Mos of dem dere jus ordinary peoples.

Well bout dis Josephine

my Uncle he say when dat woman he leave Chi Kaw Chi

no one he even miss him.

He was like dat woman he was never here.

An yet all of us

we all talk bout him like he was somebody we all

knowed real good.

Like me.

I never knowed him but I soun like I do

I can even seed him.

Dats funny issn it?

How dem peoples dey can leave dat kine of tinking

behine.

Well my Uncle he tell me

Mary Yellow Kettle an George L'Hirondelle

dey was going to dah town one night.

Mary him

he was real sick an he have to see dah doctor.

George he have an ole Hudson in dem days

one of dem great big cars.

He buy it after dah war wit dah money hees Mudder he

save for him.

George

he really like dat car an he takes good care of it.

He drive it real slow

an he polish it all dah time.

Well I guess he should

cause dat car he make him good money.

He use it for a taxi.

Dats how come he was travelling wit Mary.

In dem days you know

dat George he don believe on nutting.

Not even dah Jesus.

Dey say dat happen if you ever been in dah war.

Dah mans dat go dere

dey say dah war he was jus plain hell

an dat no good God he would let peoples do dat to

each udder.

My Uncle he say

dat George he tell him

dey was all jus superstiches when dey talk bout

Rou Garous Cheepies an dah Jesus Chrise.

Well let me tell you

dis was dah night

dat change dah way George L'Hirondelle he tink.

Him an Mary

dey was driving along an dey jus pass dah lake

an dey was climbing dah long hill

when Mary he seed an animal running along dah ridge.

He was too dark to see him good

but dey decide he mus be dah bear my Uncle Tommy he

seed dah day before.

When dey get to dah top of dah hill

dat animal he run into dah poplar bluff an dey can

see it no more.

George him

he tell my Uncle

dat he tinks dat bear he shore run damn funny

but he forget bout him

cause dey was starting down dah hill an he gots to

pay attention

cause dat hill he was very dangerous you know.

He have a big curve at dah bottom

an lots of peoples dey have bad accidents dere.

Well all of a sudden George he say

dah brakes dey stop working.

He say he yell at Mary to hang on

an he try to steer dah bes he could.

Well I guess he was going full speed when Mary he

scream.

George he look up

an dis big animal he jump right in front of dah

car an all he can member when he hit it

was dat it was a woman dat look at him.

He say he try to keep dah car on dah road

but it en up in dah ditch right up agains a bunch of

willows.

Dey wasen hurt

but Mary him

he was crying hard cause he was damn scare.

George he jump out of dah car

he wan to see what he hit.

He say him too he was scare

but hees a brave man so he get out.

You know George he tell my Uncle

dat dere was no woman on dat road

but dere was a big black wolf.

He say dat wolf he was trying to get up an when

he start to walk towards him

dat wolf he kine of cry a little bit

an he drag himself off dah road.

Jus as he head for dah bush

George he yell,

"Josephine!"

an dat wolf he turn aroun an look at at him.

You know dat George he swear on dah Prees hees book

dat when dah wolf he look at him

it was Josephine.

S. Farrell Racette '94

"No one can tell I don see dat" George he say.
"No one, not even my Mudder.
Dat wolf he was Josephine an me
I'm never gonna forget dat as long as I live."

When he go back to dah car
Mary him he won get out cause
he was too scare so dey stay dere all night.

An all night
dey can hear dat wolf kine of half howling.
George him
he say hees hairs dey jus stan up
cause he never heered dat kine of soun before.

When dah morning he comes
dey walk back to Alex Moran hees house
an Alex him
he bring hees team an he pull dah car back on dah
road.
Alex he say dere was blood an fur all over dah road
an dere was even blood on dah car.
When George he tell him what he see
Alex him he believe
cause dat man he believe on dah Rou Garous
an all dem dark tings.

Well George an Alex

dey decide right dere dat dere gonna do someting

cause dis is not dah firs time

someone he seed dis wolf

but hees dah firs time someone seed a woman.

Dey go to dah store where dey knowed all dah mans

dey'll be

an Chi Kaw Chee he was dere too.

George he tell dah mans to come over to hees house

dat night

cause him hees gonna have a poker game.

Dey know Chi Kaw Chee he'll come

cause Josephine him

he likes to play poker an hees a damn good poker

player too.

Dats dah udder ting!

Me I nearly forget.

Dem Rou Garous when dere in dah peoples body

dey like to play poker.

Dats right

Dey like to play poker.

Well dat Chi Kaw Chee

he tell dem he'll come for shore

but Josephine he can come cause

he hurt hisself trying to get dah chickens down from

dah hayloft.

On dah way home George an Alex dey make a plan.

Alex him

he'll keep dah mans busy playing poker

an George him

he'll go to Chi Kaw Chee hees house

an he'll look trough dah window an prove dat

Josephine hees a Rou Garou.

Dat night when Chi Kaw Chee he get dere

an all dah mans dey was playing

George he go over to hees house

an he look in dah window.

He say dat Josephine he was packing a suitcase an

when he turn aroun

George he say

dat woman was all black an blue.

George he say

he was standing a long ways from dah house

underneet some trees

but when dat Josephine he look up

he say

dat woman look him right in dah eyes an

George he can move.

He say he feel jus paralize an he turn cole all over.

"Boy!" he say.

"Dah hairs on my neck dey stan straight up

an my belly he jus feel sick."

Dah only udder time he feel like dat

he tell my Uncle

was when he was in dah war

an he come out of dah trench an he seed dah dead

mans all over.

He say it was dah firs time he knowed he was part of

someting dat was evil

an tonight he was dah secon time.

George he say

he make dah sign of dah cross

an for dah firs time in many years

he call dah Jesus an dah Virgin Mary.

Well dah next morning real early

Chi Kaw Chee he come to George hees house

an he tell him Josephine he leave him.

"All hees clos dere gone" he say

an he start to cry.

Chi Kaw Chee you know

he love dat woman.

He love him a lot.

He was never dah same after dat happen.

He become jus pitiful.

He live alone all hees life an at night

he walk dah ridges looking for dat woman.

An George him

he start going to dah church an he never tell dah

peoples again

dat dey was superstiches.

But you know my Mudder

he was real mad when I tell him what Tommy he tell

me.

He say dah Prees he win again an he give anudder

woman a bad name

jus to make good Catlics of dah peoples.

My Mudder he say

Josephine he was a good woman an

George he was jus a stupid man.

An me too

my Mudder he say

I was gonna end up stupid if I listen to dem kine of stories.

My Mudder you know

he always look after Chi Kaw Chee

feeding him an making dah mans look for him if he don

come back in dah morning.

My Mudder you know

he was a good woman an he have dah seeing.

But me

I don know.

I jus never know who hees right

my Mudder or dah mans an dah Prees.

Ole Arcand

he was a big strong man.

He stan well over six feet tall

an he weigh damn near two hundred pounds.

He was a good lookin man too.

All dem ole Halfbreeds dey was good lookin.

Ole Arcand

he gots long hair an a big moostache

an real shiny eyes

jus like he know someting you don know bout

like he was laughin all dah time.

He use to wear dem ole fashion clothes

even after we could afford dah new kine.

He wear dem baggy pants

dah ole Breeds dey use to wear.

Dey was wool I guess.

He wear dem moosehide leggins too

dey come up to dah knees

an dah shirts wit dah big sleeves.

He have a beaded velvet vest

an he always wear a Red River sash an a flat crown hat.

BOY

he was a good lookin ole man.

Us kids we use to like him

he always have time to stop an talk wit us.

I member he use to hold up dat sash

an tell me an Frank,

dats my younger brudder,

dat dis was our culture.

We don speak Anglais very good in dem days

jus kind of a Halfbreed mixture

so we never understan dat word culture.

But boy!

He shore sounds good dat word real important.

Us Halfbreeds

we don have much to feel important bout in dem days.

I guess dats why we use to love him so much dat ole man.

He make us feel like we got someting.

Dat sash he was bright

you can see him for a long ways.

I member me an Frank

we work like hell trapping rats so we can have one.

When we finely gots enough money

we went to see him.

We figure he knows where we can get dem.

Boy

he shore look sad when we show him our money

an we tell him we wan two.

"Hey hey noosimuk" he says

"We can buy dem no more."

Well me an Frank

we shore feel bad cause you know

we work all spring trapping so we can buy dem.

We wan to wear dis culture too.

Well you know

he tell us dat after da big fight at Batoche.

Dah one where Mooshoom Gabe

he organize all da Halfbreeds an dey get Louis Riel?

Well dat time.

I guess after dey take Riel

dah soldiers dey catch up to dah peoples dat was running away

an dey take all dere guns an bullets.

An dah soldiers

dey take dah sashes too.

Boy dats funny issn it?

why would dey take dah sashes?

Well anyways

none of dah stores dey sell dem

an we gots no sheeps.

So we gots no wool to make dem ourselves.

Dere was nutting me an Frank we could do

so we give our Mudder dah money instead.

We was purdy hard up in dose days

it was jus after my Dad he die

so my Mudder he could shore use it.

Well you know

dis Ole Arcand

he was one hell of a fiddle player.

Boy he can play anyting

an he makes up hees own songs too.

He always have a good story bout how he got dah

song.

He say he got one song from dah wind at Batoche

anudder one

he say dat his horse he give it to him.

But one good song he have

dat was dah bes one of all.

He call dat one La Beau Sha Shoo.

He tell us he die.

Dat ole man

he was always dying an going to dah heaven

an when he come back

he gots a new song.

Even dah ole peoples

dey don know if hees telling dah troot or not

cause he shore come back wit some good songs.

No one on dis earth

hees smart enough to give dem to him.

Anyways in dis story

bout La Beau Sha Shoo

he tell it he got sick.

Boy

I guess he gots real sick.

Five days an five nights he says.

Finely his ole lady

she gets dah Prees

an he give um hees last rites.

Ole Arcand he say dat night

after hees wife an hees sons dey go to sleep

he start to float

an he float up to dah heaven.

I guess he never even stop at dah gate

he jus went inside an he land on hees feet.

Boy

he say

he was shore a nice place.

Dah road he look like pure silver

an dere was all kines of nice flowers an trees.

He say he start walking

an bout half a mile up dah road

he see dah Jesus Chrise sitting along side dah road.

Dah Jesus he says to him

"Sit down Jonas an have a drink wit me."

Dey have wine in heaven you know

Ole Arcand he says "Tapwe anima!"

Dah Jesus he poured me a big glass full

an boy

he was a nice glass too!

He was all gold

wit diamonds an green an red stones.

So me I have a drink wit him.

Ole Arcand say

"Who am I to say no to dah Jesus Chrise."

Jesus he tell me
Ole Arcand say
"Jonas I'm shore glad you come here for a visit
cause not many peoples aroun here dey'll drink wit me.
Dere all scare of my ole man."

"I'm not visiting" Ole Arcand he tell him.
"I die. I come here to live."

Well
dah Jesus he got purdy excited
I guess he damn near spill hees wine.

He call Gabriel over.
You know
dah one he looks after dah gate?
Well him an dah Jesus dey look in dah big book.

Ole Arcand he says
Ole Gabriel him
he kinda look like dah Prees back home
He wears dem round glasses like dat.

I guess Ole Gabe
He look at him over hees glasses an he say
"Jonas your not in dah book. Your jus visiting."

"Oh tank God," dah Jesus say

an he make dah sign of dah cross.

Ole Arcand

he say dah Jesus he was purdy scared for a minute.

"I never argue wit him."

Ole Arcand he say, "I got lots of work to do.

My boys dey was too young yet to run dah farm.

But me I don wan to go home yet," he says,

"Dah Jesus he still got a half a jug of wine."

Well he see me lookin at it an he says

"Here Jonas

we'll finish dis jug firs before you go home."

Ole Arcand he say

dah Jesus he fill dah glass again.

But Ole Gabe him

I guess he don like dat very much.

"So dah Jesus he tell him to go back to dah gate

An preten he don see nutting."

Boy

Ole Arcand say

when Ole Gabe he leave

dey did some serious drinking.

"You know Jonas" dah Jesus say

"Your a damned good fiddle player.

Me I always wan to play dah fiddle

But I never have a chance.

When da Lucifer he get kicked out

he take all dah fiddles wit him an all we got now is harps.

But me Jonas

I got a hell of a song I been hearing in my head.

I'll give it to you

an you learn to play it when you get home."

Ole Arcand he says him an dah Jesus

dey finish dah wine an dah Jesus

he make mouth music an teach him dis song.

You know

Ole Arcand he always stop hees story here

an he take his fiddle out of dah flour sack

where he keep him an he would start playing.

Ooh

he was a hell of a song!

He was kinda wile

full of high stepping an growling

an we could shore dance to him.

An when he finish playing

He would look at us an say,

"Yes Sir dah Jesus Chrise he give me dis song."

He say "Jonas you call dis song La Beau Sha Shoo

an you play it for all dah peoples when you get home."

BIG JOHN

In dah ole days dah Indians
dey use to get a bad time from dah
Indian Department.
Dey still do I guess
but hees not as bad as he use to be.
Dey got dere edjication now
an dey know dere rights.
But in dah ole days
he wasen like dat. Oh no!
He was very different.

My ole Uncle Big John
he was a Treaty. He was a real smart man
an very kine too.
He was one of dem peoples dat take pictures
an he develop dem hees own self.
He have a black room he call it in hees cellar
an when he takes pictures
he goes down dere an he develope dem.

Ooh he was a very smart man dat one.
He learn how to do dat you know
from a book he sen away for in dah States.

Well not him!

I nearly forget dat

cause him he don got an edjication.

He was a little girl

Big John an my Auntie dey raise.

Gorsh

me I jus can member dat little girl hees name.

Boy me

I'm getting bad for dat you know.

Forgetting every damn ting.

Anyways

dat little girl he go to dah residential school

an when he come home for dah holidays

he read dah newspapers for Big John.

Dats where dey see dis book for picture taking.

So Big John him

he get dat little girl to sen some money

to dah States.

When dah picture stuff he come

dat little girl

he read dah struction book out loud

an Big John he start making pictures

an he never quit.

All dah pictures we got in our family
an jus bout all dah ones dah Indians dey gots
in Ahtakakoop
my Uncle Big John he take dem.

Dat man he take pictures of every damn ting.
Peoples, animals, flowers.
He take dat camera every place he goes.

An you know
in all dem pictures we gots
Big John him
hees standing right in dah middle.
Ooh he was a very smart man
an very kine too.

But you know
dat Indian Department he don like him.
Dey never treat him wit respec
dah way everybody else he do.
I guess dey don like nobody to be smarter den dem.
Not in dem days anyway.

I member one time
I was bout twelve years ole I guess.
I go wit him to see dah Farm Instructor.

My Uncle

he wans to kill one of hees cows

cause him an hees family dey was real hard up.

Well you know

dat Farm Instructor he was a Halfbreed.

Jus like me

I was a Halfbreed too.

But dat man he was very different.

Dat one he act real smart.

He ask Big John what for he wan to kill hees cows.

Big John he tell him

he don wan to kill all hees cows

he jus wan to kill a steer.

Cause him he gots no food to feed hees family.

Well dat Farm Instructor he tell him to go hunting.

Dats how stupid dat man he was.

He know damn well Big John he have to put hees

crop in an he gots no time to hunt.

Anyways

Big John he don have no gun eeder an even if he

did where would he get shells.

Nobody he could afford shells in dose days.

All dah peoples dey was pour.

An besides

My Uncle he stop hunting when he decide

hees gonna be a farmer.

Dats right.

Cause dats what dah Indian Department he wans all

dah Indians to do.

An my Uncle him

he really believe dat all dah peoples dey gotta

learn dis new way of living.

He believe wit all hees heart

dat if dah peoples dey learn dah new ways

den he'll be easier for all dah kids.

An Big John him

he was a man dat always tink bout dah kids.

Well!

Dat Farm Instructor you tink he own dat damn

reservation he act so smart.

He tell my Uncle Big John

hees never gonna be a farmer

if he keeps on killing hees cows.

He talk to him like a kid dat don know nutting.

Me

I can hardly believe what I hear him say

cause I knowed dat man real good.

I knowed hees family too.

An none of dem

including him

knowed a damn ting bout farming.

None of dem was ever any good for anyting.

How he ever get dat job

nobody he knows.

All dey was ever good for my Mudder he use to say

was to give dah res of us Breeds a bad name.

Dats true you know

dere was some peoples dey was like dat in dem days.

Jus plain no good.

Well anyways

when he finish giving my Uncle a big talk

he say

"No Big John I can give you pimmishion to kill dah

Kings Cows.

Dah King he give you dem cows so you can learn to be

civilize like us."

Dat damn shit.

I don know where he learn dat word "civilize."

All dem cows

dey belongs to dah Indians

not dat damn King dat nobody he ever seed.

Dat Halfbreed you know

he must of heerd somebody use dat word "civilize"

an hees so stupid him he have to use it too.

Me

I'm damn shore

he don know what dah hell dat word he mean

cause none of us peoples we use dem kine of words.

We was civilize

cause me

I learn when I get older

dat word

he mean somebody hees got good manners

an hees got respec for his ownself

an udder peoples.

An dats someting dat man he shore as hell don got.

Well my Uncle him
he get so mad he was gonna hit him
an you know he was a big man my Uncle.
Not dah kine you fool wit dats for shore.

Well
dat Farm Instructor he gets real scared
an he run behine dah table.
"You get dah hell out of here Big John" he yell.
"Or I'll report you to dah Mounties an you'll go to
dah jail."

Well my Uncle him
he come to hees senses damn quick
cause he don wan to go to dah jail so we go home
an when we get dere
Big John he grab dah axe.
Far as hees concern
dah King an dat Farm Instructor
dey can go to hell
he was gonna kill dat cow.

My Auntie him
he gets real scared.
He cry an he beg Big John not to do it
cause dah Mounties dey might kill him
like dey done to Almighty Voice over at One Arrows
reservation.

Dat was over a cow too you know.

Almighty Voice him

he kill a cow wit no pimmishion

cause dey was starving

an dah Farm Instructor he report him.

Well dah Mounties dey trowed him in dah jail an

dey tell him dey was going to hang him.

Well

what dat man he was suppose to do?

He run away of course.

Me too I'd run away if somebody he say dey was gonna hang me.

I'd be a damn fool if I don.

So dats what Almighty Voice he do

an he stay hiding for two years I tink

den dey fine him.

Dey come wit a whole bunch of policemans an white

mans to help dem

all from dis country too.

Some of dem mans dat do dat

dere ancestors dere our neighbours now.

Dat shore is funny issn it what peoples dey'll do?

Anyways

dey kill Almighty Voice over a damn cow.

Hees jus not right how dey can do dat.

Jus kill a man for killing hees own cow.

Dats how bad dat Indian Department he use to be in

dem days.

Well my Uncle

he listen to my Aunty.

Dey gots two kids you know

an who hees gonna look after dem if he goes to dah

jail or

maybe ends up dead?

Dat night

we gots no food for supper

so me an my Uncle

we make ourselves bows an arrows early in dah

morning

we go hunting.

We have to go a long ways cause dah game he was

scarce.

An you know

I hate to say dis cause I love my Uncle very much

an I have respec for him

he was a smart man

but he shore wasen much of a hunter.

He was a damn good ting

me I know someting bout hunting

cause bout ten o'clock in dah morning

I get two ducks.

Big John he really brag me.

He use to do dat all dah time you know

make you feel good for doing someting.

But I tell you

if it wasen for ole Mooshoom Peekeekoot

dat teach me to hunt

me

I probley wouldn get nutting.

But I was a kid den

don know any better

so I act like I do dis all dah time

instead of being happy dat dah good God he was kine

to me dat morning.

On dah way home

my Uncle he tell me I was lucky I wasen a Treaty.

Well me

I don know if I agree wit him or not.

Cause I shore don tink being a Halfbreed was very

good eeder.

Us Halfbreeds we don ever got land.

An we shore as hell got no Kings cows to kill.

Me you know

I never wan to be a Treaty.

I see how bad dey was treated.

I see my Uncle

a big strong man, a real smart man

treated worse den a dog an it hurt me inside.

At leas us Breeds

nobody hees hired to treat us like dat.

An we was our own bosses too.

Well in dem days anyways

I can say dat bout today.

He seems like everybody hees dah boss over us now.

But not long time ago.

Long time ago

we was jus left alone

an I tink he was better dat way.

Well dat Farm Instructor you know

I never forget him.

When I growed up an become a man

I give him one hell of a lickin.

But it don make me feel very good.

Dat kine of man

a lickin hees too good for him.

Me

I jus never understan dem kine of peoples.

Boy

when I get married an have a family of my own

an dey was ole enough to understand

I tell dem

"If any one of youse ever work for dah government

agains your own peoples

don ever come home again."

Dats dah worse sin as far as I'm concern

to work agains your own peoples.

Well I'm an Ole man now

I'm still a Halfbreed

an I'm still pour.

But me

I'm proud to say

none of my kids dey ever done dat

an I know Big John him too

he'd be damn proud.

Ooh

he was a good ole man

an real smart too.

He end up being a big farmer you know

but dere all gone now.

Big John

him an hees two kids dey die in dah flu epidemic.

An my Aunty

he die a few years ago. He was 112.

Hees name he was Quaychich

an dat one too he have a good story.

Next time

I'll tell you bout him.

JACOB

Mistupuch he was my Granmudder.

He come from Muskeg

dat was before he was a reservation.

My Granmudder he was bout twenty-eight when he

marry my Granfawder.

Dat was real ole for a woman to marry in dem days.

But he was an Indian doctor

I guess dats why he wait so long.

Ooh he was a good doctor too.

All the peoples dey say dat bout him.

He doctor everybody dat come to him

an he birt all dah babies too.

Jus bout everybody my age

My Granmudder he birt dem.

He marry my Granfawder aroun 1890.

Dat ole man he come to him for doctoring

an when he get better

he never leave him again.

Dey get married dah Indian way

an after dat my Granfawder

he help him wit all hees doctoring.

Dats dah way he use to be a long time ago.

If dah woman he work
den dah man he help him an if dah man he work
dah woman he help.
You never heerd peoples fighting over whose job he was
dey all know what dey got to do to stay alive.

My Granfawder his name he was Kannap
but dah whitemans dey call him "Jim Boy"
so hees Indian name he gets los.
Dats why we don know who his peoples dey are.
We los lots of our relations like dat.
Dey get dah whitemans name
den no body
he knows who his peoples dey are anymore.

Sometimes me
I tink dats dah reason why we have such a hard time
us peoples.
Our roots dey gets broken so many times.
Hees hard to be strong you know
when you don got far to look back for help.

Dah whitemans
he can look back for thousands of years
cause him
he write everyting down.

But us peoples

we use dah membering

an we pass it on by telling stories an singing songs.

Sometimes we even dance dah membering.

But all dis trouble you know

he start after we get dah new names

he come a new language an a new way of living.

Once a long time ago

I could'ave told you dah story of my Granfawder Kannap

an all his peoples but no more.

All I can tell you now

is bout Jim Boy

an hees story hees not very ole.

Well my Granmudder Mistupuch

he never gets a whitemans name an him

he knowed lots of stories.

Dat ole lady

he even knowed dah songs.

He always use to tell me

one bout an ole man call Jacob.

Dat ole man you know

he don live too far from here.

Well hees gone now

but dis story he was bout him when he was alive.

Jacob him

he gets one of dem new names when dey put him in dah

residential school.

He was a jus small boy when he go

an he don come home for twelve years.

Twelve years!

Dats a long time to be gone from your peoples.

He can come home you know

cause dah school he was damn near two hundred miles

away.

His Mommy an Daddy dey can go an see him

cause deres no roads in dem days

an dah Indians dey don gots many horses

specially to travel dat far.

Dats true you know

not many peoples in dem days dey have horses.

Its only in dah comic books an dah picture shows dey

gots lots of horses.

He was never like dat in dah real life.

Well Jacob him

he stay in dat school all dem years an when he come

home he was a man.

While he was gone

his Mommy an Daddy dey die so he gots nobody.

An on top of dat

nobody he knowed him cause he gots a new name.

My Granmudder

he say dat ole man he have a hell of time.

Nobody he can understand dat

unless he happen to him.

Dem peoples dat go away to dem schools

an come back you know dey really suffer.

No matter how many stories we tell

we'll never be able to tell

what dem schools dey done to dah peoples

an all dere relations.

Well anyways

Jacob he was jus plain pitiful.

He can talk his own language.

He don know how to live in dah bush.

Its a good ting da peoples dey was kine

cause dey help him dah very bes dey can.

Well a couple of summers later

he meet dis girl

an dey gets married.

Dat girl he was kine

an real smart too.

He teach Jacob how to make an Indian living.

Dey have a good life togedder an after a few years

dey have a boy.

Not long after dat

dey raise two little girls dat was orphans.

Jacob an his wife dey was good peoples.

Boat of dem dey was hard working

an all dah peoples

dey respec dem an dey come to Jacob for advice.

But dah good times dey was too good to las

cause one day

dah Preeses

dey comes to dah village wit dah policemans.

Dey come to take dah kids to dah school.

When dey get to Jacob hees house

he tell dem dey can take his kids.

Dah Prees he tell him

he have to lets dem go cause dats the law.

Well dah Prees

he have a big book

an dat book he gots dah names

of all dah kids

an who dey belongs to.

He open dat book an ask Jacob for his name
an den he look it up.
"Jacob" he say
"you know better you went to dah school an you know
dah edjication hees important."

My Granmudder Mistupuch
he say Jacob he tell that Prees
"Yes I go to dah school
an dats why I don wan my kids to go.
All dere is in dat place is suffering."

Dah Prees he wasen happy bout dat
an he say to Jacob
"But the peoples dey have to suffer Jacob
cause dah Jesus he suffer."

"But dah Jesus he never lose his language an
hees peoples" Jacob tell him.
"He stay home in hees own land an he do hees
suffering."

Well da Prees him
he gets mad
an he tell him its a sin to tink like dat
an hees gonna end up in purgatory for dem kind of
words.

But Jacob he don care
cause far as hees concern
purgatory
he can be worse den the hell he live wit trying to
learn hees language an hees Indian ways.

He tell dat Prees
he don even know who his people dey are.
"Dah Jesus he knowed his Mommy an Daddy"
Jacob he tell him
"an he always knowed who his people dey are."

Well
dah Prees he tell him
if he wans to know who hees peoples dey are
he can tell him dat
an he open in dah book again.

"Your Dad hees Indian name he was Awchak"
dah prees he say
"I tink dat means Star in your language.
He never gets a new name cause he never become a
Christian."

Jacob he tell my Granmudder
dat when da Prees he say hees Dad hees name
his wife he start to cry real hard.

"Jacob someday you'll tank the God we done dis."

dah Prees he tell him

an dey start loading up dah kids on dah big wagons.

All dah kids dey was crying an screaming

an dah mudders

dey was chasing dah wagons.

Dah ole womans

dey was all singing dah det song

an none of the mans

dey can do anyting.

Dey can

cause the policemans dey gots guns.

When dah wagons dey was all gone

Jacob he look for hees wife but he can find him no

place.

An ole woman he see him an he call to him

"Pay api noosim."

"Come an sit down my grandchild I mus talk to you.

Hees hard for me to tell you dis but dat Prees

hees book he bring us bad news today.

He tell you dat Awchak he was your Daddy.

My grandchild

Awchak he was your wife's Daddy too."

S. Farrell Racette '94

Jacob he tell my Granmudder
he can cry when he hear dat.
He can even hurt inside.
Dat night he go looking
an he fine hees wife in dah bush.
Dat woman he kill hisself.

Jacob he say
dah ole womans
dey stay wit him for a long time
an dey sing healing songs an dey try to help him
but he say he can feel nutting.
Maybe if he did
he would have done dah same ting.

For many years Jacob he was like dat
jus dead inside.

Dah peoples dey try to talk wit him
but it was no use.
Hees kids dey growed up
an dey come home an live wit him.
"I made dem suffer" he tell my Granmudder.
"Dem kids dey try so hard to help me."

Den one day
his daughter he get married an he have a baby.
He bring it to Jacob to see.

Jacob he say

he look at dat lil baby

an he start to cry an he can stop.

He say he cry for himself an his wife

an den he cry for his Mommy an Daddy.

When he was done

he sing dah healing songs dah ole womans

dey sing to him a long time ago.

Well you know

Jacob he die when he was an ole ole man.

An all hees life

he write in a big book

dah Indian names of all dah Mommies an Daddies.

An beside dem

he write dah ole names an

dah new names of all dere kids.

An for dah res of hees life

he fight dah government to build schools on the

reservation.

"The good God he wouldn of make babies come

from Mommies an Daddies,"

he use to say,

"if he didn wan dem to stay home

an learn dere language

an dere Indian ways."

You know

dat ole man was right.

Nobody he can do dat.

Take all dah babies away. Hees jus not right.

Long time ago

dah ole peoples dey use to do dah naming

an dey do dah teaching too.

If dah parents dey have troubles

den dah aunties an dah uncles

or somebody in dah family

he help out till dah parents dey gets dere life work

out.

But no one

no one

he ever take dah babies away from dere peoples.

You know my ole Granmudder

Mistupuch

he have lots of stories bout people like Jacob.

Good ole peoples

dat work hard so tings will be better for us.

We should never forget dem ole peoples.

Joseph's Justice

You know dah big fight at Batoche?

Dah one where we fight dah Anglais?

Well dat one.

Dis story he happen den

an dah name of dah man is Joseph.

He was a Halfbreed guy

An he don take part in dat war.

Dere was lots of mans like dat in dem days.

Dey wasen scare of dah Anglais

or dah government.

Oh No!

Dey jus wasen interest in fighting for land

or edjication

cause dey don believe dat Anglais government

hees gonna give dem anyting.

So

dey jus mine dere own business.

Deres lots of peoples like dat

even today.

Dey jus like to stick to demselves dats all.

Well shore

some of dem dey was cowards

an udder ones jus plain lazy.

But most of dem

dey jus got no believing dats all.

Dis Joseph

he was one of dem dat don believe.

He was jus minding hees own business

trapping an working for hees ownself

while dah udder mans dey was fighting dah war.

An den dah war he was over

an our peoples dey lose.

Dah Anglais General he take Louis

an dah udder mans to Regina

where hees gonna put dem in dah jail so dey can go to

dah court.

Of cours he never got all of dem

jus Louis

cause Louis him

he give hees self up.

Dah udder ones

dey was capture but not Gabriel dough.

Oh no!

Him an Michel Dumas

dey run away to dah States an hide.

Ooh Gabe him

he die before he give hisself up.

Dats dah kine of mans he was.

Louis him

he was differen.

Differen from Gabe an all dah udders.

I guess you can say he was a spirit man.

He give hisself to dah peoples

an he do dat when he was a small boy.

Hees Daddy you know

he was dat kine of mans too.

He put dah peoples before hees family even.

Dere's not many mans you know

dere born like dat.

Yeah dat Louis

he give us anudder kine of membering.

But not Gabe.

Hoo

he was a wile tough mans him.

He was dah kine of mans he can make you believe you

can do anyting on dis eart

long as you was tough enough to stan on your feet.

But you know dis Joseph

dah one I'm telling dah story bout?

He was jus ordinary.

Ordinary Halfbreed like us.

Not dah kine of mans anyone he tell stories bout.

Well dere he was him

minding hees own business

when dah General he win dah war an he comes riding by

wit hees Halfbreed prisoners.

Joseph he say he was walking home wit hees gun an

hees beaver pelts

when dah soldiers dey see him.

He say dey was making a hell of a racket.

Celebrating I guess

cause dey win dah war.

Dey damn near scare him to det he say.

Well dem soldiers

soon as dey see him

dey grab him an dey haul him to dah General.

Well my ole Uncle

hees name he was Alcid

hees dah one who tell me dis story.

He say dat Anglais General

he was riding a big white horse dat dance all dah time.

An dat horse

he was dancing all over when dah soldiers dey bring

Joseph to him.

An dem soldiers

dey trowed Joseph right in front of dat dancing

horse.

SHERRY FARRELL RACETTE '94

Well Joseph he tell my Uncle

he jump up as fas as he can.

He don wan to get step on.

An den

dat horse he start bucking an he buck dat General

right off.

I guess dat Anglais horse

he never smell a Halfbreed trapper before.

When dat General he finely get dat horse to settle

down

he tell Joseph

"Batoche he fall an your leader

Louis Riel he surrender.

Him an all dese mans dere under arres. An you my good

man, your under arres too."

"If I'm a good man" Joseph he say to him

"den what for you arres me?"

Dah General he don like dat very much an he say

"Dah charge hees high treason."

Joseph him

he don know what dat word treason he mean

but he say

it soun awful dangerous

so he talk real careful

jus in case hees got someting to do wit shooting.

Dem soldiers you know

dey got guns an he say

dey look like dey wan to use dem.

Joseph you know

him he don trus dah Anglais.

He never trus dem in hees whole life.

Well dah General he yell at dah soldiers to put

Joseph in dah wagon wit dah udder mans.

So dah soldiers dey put chains on him

an dey trowed him in dah wagon.

Joseph he say

dah Halfbreeds an dah Indians dey was all chained togedder.

Some of dem

dey was on dah wagons an some of dem dey was walking.

He say he look for Louis

but he can see him no wheres.

Maybe he was in a cover wagon

cause he was dah leader

an dey don wan nobody to see him or talk to him.

But Joseph

he say he knowed dah udder mans.

Dere was ole Parenteau

he was wearing chains like an outlaw.

Dat ole man he can hurt nobody, hees over eighty

years ole.

An dere was dah Vandal boys

an one of dah Arcands.

Even hees brudder-ing-law Moise Tourond he was

dere.

Boy he say

dey look rough.

He was raining an real cole an all dey was wearing

was raggy ole clothes.

Some of dem dey don even got no shoes.

An lots of dem dey was wounded

an all of dem

dey was real hungry.

Well Joseph him

he tink he better try an say someting

cause dis whole damn ting

hees starting to look pretty damn scary.

An him

he wan dem to know he wasen mix up in it.

Well he try talking to dem soldiers but dey don even
listen to him.
He start hollering an yelling
but hees brudder-ing-law Moise
he tell him to shut up
cause nobody he gives a damn if hees guilty or not
anyways.

Well
it took dem a long time to get to Regina
an when dey get dere
dey was trowed in dah jail.
Joseph him
he was dere for six monts before he come up for trial.
An when he do
he tell dah Judge what he happen to him
an dat Judge he believe on him an he let him go.

But Joseph him
he wan hees gun an hees furs back
an he ask for dem.
He say dah Judge an all dah government peoples
dey jus laugh at him
an dey tell him
he should be grateful he don get hanged or go to
Stony Mountain Jail.

Well he leave dere

an he go to dah policemans.

Dey tell him he should jus forget bout it an get

dah hell home as fas as he can.

But dat Joseph you know

he was a real hard headed mans

not dah kine dat give up jus like dat.

An he tell dem policemans

dat if it was him dat steal from dah General

he would of got charge.

An him

he never even done nutting

an hees dah one dat gets treated like a crimnal.

Finely

my ole Uncle he say

one of dah policemans he gets tired of him

an he say

"Okey Joseph. You can press charges. But me I

shore hope you know what your doing cause dis is

goana be one hell of a mess before hees over."

Well

it took a long time before dey go to dah court.

An when he gets dere

Joseph he meet dis lawyer

an dis lawyer

he ask him what hees doing dere.

When Joseph he tell him
dat lawyer he laugh like hell an he tell Joseph
he'll help him.
Dat lawyer he was an Irishman
an dem Irish you know
dey don like dah Anglais eeder.

My ole Uncle Alcid
he say
dem Irish
dey was dah only ones dat really try to help us in dem days.
I guess dats because dah Anglais dey take all dere lan too.

Well
Joseph he lose in dah court in Regina but he knowed
he wouldn win dere
cause Regina
he was an Anglais town.

So him an dat lawyer
dey take it to dah high court.
Again he took a long time
but finely he heered.
Dat General
he was foun guilty for stealing.

You know dey say everybody he steal in dah war time.
But hees agains dah law you know.
Dats true.

Dah soldiers dere suppose to honour cause dey belongs

to dah Queen.

Well at Batoche dem soldiers

dey eeder don know dat or dey gots no respec for dere Queen

cause all of dem dey steal.

Not jus from Joseph eeder

dey steal from all dah peoples.

Dah Halfbreeds

dey wasen rich you know

dey jus gots a few little nice tings.

When dem soldiers come

dey chase dah peoples away

an dey go into dere howses

an dey clean dem out.

Dey even burn some of dah howses to dah groun.

Dey do dat to Gabe hees house you know.

Burn it to dah groun.

Too damn bad nobody else he press charges agains dem.

Well Joseph him

he won hees case an dah General he don look so good.

But Joseph

he don get no compensation from no one.

He never even get hees gun back.

Well he really get mad den.

Whats dah damn use of winning if you don get your

stuff back?

He don care if dah General he look good or bad

all he wan

is hees gun an hees furs back.

Well he don know what hees gonna do now

cause dat General he leave our country not long after

dah court.

He go back to hees own country in Angleterre.

Dere dah Queen he make him a gentlemans.

You know dah kine dat wear dah armor.

An dah Queen he even put him in charge of all hees

jools.

Dat General

he become a hell of a hero for putting down dah

Breeds at Batoche.

Fars I'm concern

he don have much to brag bout.

Five tousan of dem an less den a hundred of us.

Oh I know dah history books dey say we was two

hundred an fifty.

But you gotta member

dey write dah history books.

My ole Uncle Alcid

he was dere

an he say dere was less den a hundred at Batoche.

An mos of dem

dey was ole mans.

Well never mine bout dat

cause Joseph him

he don care anyways.

All he wan is hees gun an hees furs.

So he go to dah court again.

Dis time hees dah high court in Angleterre

an over dere he gets in dah newspaper an dem Anglais

dey write all bout it.

Dat really help him you know.

But dats shore funny how he is.

Dey like dah Breeds over dere

but dey hate dem here.

Me I jus never can figure out dem Anglais.

Well dat Irish lawyer he win dah case for Joseph.

An in dah court

he make a hell of a fool out of dah General

at lees

dats what all dah ole mans dey say.

Jimmy Isbister

he use to say dat too

cause he read dah newspapers dat come from over

dere.

Dat Jimmy you know

he was well edjicated.

He was one of dah mans dat go wit Gabe to Montana to

get Louis.

He was a smart man dat Jimmy

he understan dah Anglais.

He was a Scotch Halfbreed

an hees Daddy

he sen him to Angleterre to get hees edjication.

Dah newspapers over dere

dey say Joseph he win hees case an he gets compensation

for hees gun an furs.

Dey say he gets fifteen hundred dollars!

Boy dats a hell of a pile of money in dem days.

An you know dat general dey say he retire "in disgrace."

Me I'm not shore what dat mean but I tink

he means he was shamed

an dey say dat dah Queen he take away hees job guarding dah palace jools.

If dats true den dat was a good ting

cause a man dats a leader he should have more respec.

Like Louis he have lots of respec.

Me I always like dah story bout Joseph.

Cause you know

maybe we lose dah war

but one man he win

cause him he believe on hisself

an he don give up.

Dat kine of man hees real important.

Jus as important as Louis an Gabe

cause hees story

he tell you a little bit bout how our peoples dey

was like in dem days.

An dats true! Dey was strong an hardheaded.

Tanks for listening to me.

 DAH TEEF

You know
me I talk bout dah whitemans like dere dah only
ones dat steal.
But dats not true you know
cause some of our own peoples dey steal too.

Oh yeah dats true.
We gots some damn good teefs among us
an dah worse ting bout dem
is dey steal from us dere very own peoples.

I member a man one time
dat was a teef.
Boy he was a bad one too.
At firs
he wasen very good at it
an he gets caught all dah time.

Later
when he goes away from our village
he becomes perfessional
an he gets real good.
But dah peoples dey knowed it was him
cause he already build a repetation as one.

He use to steal every damn ting dat man.

He jus can be choosey.

He never gets good enough to steal land dough.

Maybe it cause we don gots any to steal by den

an he gots no practice.

But boy

he shore got good at stealing everyting else.

One time you know dis ole man

we call him Geebow.

He have a nice hat.

Hoo, he was real fancy.

A black one

dah kine da ole Breeds dey really like.

Hees got a silk embroder hatban wit a falcon fedder

stuck on it.

Dat falcon fedder you know

he was ole Geebow hees spirit

an he help him all hees life.

Well one day

dis ole Geebow he go visit Margareet.

Margareet him

he was an ole widow woman dat Geebow he like.

When he gets to hees house

dat ole lady he have a nice meal all cook

an he ask him to stay.

You know

dat ole man he never take hees hat off nearly all hees life

but when Margareet he ask him to eat

he take it off.

Dat ole Geebow

he gots good manners

like all dah ole peoples dey use to have.

Well on dis day

dis man dat was dah teef

he come visiting too.

Dat man he always knowed where dah good meals dey was.

Boy

I like to use hees name

but I can do dat cause he wouldn be right.

An me

I don wan to make hees granchildren suffer

cause dere all good peoples.

Hees not dere fault dat dere Granfawder he pick dat

way to make a name for hisself.

Anyways

dah teef he come visiting

an Margareet him

he wasen very happy bout dat cause dat mean him an

Geebow

dey can be alone.

But Margareet him

he was a good woman

so he ask him to eat wit dem

an he watch him real clos so he don steal nutting.

Dere wasen very much he can steal from dah table

anyways

cept dah knifes an forks.

An Margareet he knowed he wouldn dare take dem

cause dat woman you know

hees gots a hell of a repetation for being a hardheaded woman

when he gets mad.

Dat man he have to be a damn fool to steal from

hees table.

So dey sit down to eat

Margareet ole Geebow an dah teef.

An dey make good talk at dah table like civilize

peoples.

Hoo, he was a hell of a meal too.

Dat woman he was a good cook
an he really done hees bes for Geebow.
When dey finish eating
dah teef he jump up an he say he gots to go.
"I got to talk business wit a Frenchman called
Bilado"
He say.
Den he tank Margareet an he go.

When he leave
Margareet he check all hees knifes an forks.
Dey was all dere
but Margareet he still don trust him.
"Someting hees not right"
Margareet he say to Geebow.
"Hees not like dat man to leave when he knowed I got raisen pie."

"By golly"
Ole Geebow he say
"Maybe dah Prees he finely talk some sense into him."

Dem ole peoples
dey feel real good dat nutting he was missing
an maybe
dat man he change hees ways.

Dey visit till late at night

an ole Geebow him

he finely get dah courage to ask Margareet to marry him.

Margareet he say yes

cause hees been waiting damn near twenty years for

dat ole man to ask him.

Ooh dey have a good visit after dat.

Dey kiss

an dey talk bout dah wedding dere gonna have.

Ole Geebow him

hees never been married before an he wan to have a

big wedding.

He wans dah high mass

an everyting dat go wit it.

Margareet he like dat

cause now he can wear a long dress. He can do dat

dah firs time cause he was too pour.

Dat Margareet

he was a rich woman now cause hees husban

he use to be a big farmer

an he leave him all hees money.

Course him

he deserve dat money cause he done damn near all dah work.

But anyways dat ole Geebow

he was damn lucky dat woman he love him

an he wan to marry him.

Well finely he was eleven o' clock

time for ole Geebow to go home.

In dem days you know

nobody wit any sense he walk home at midnight or after

cause dere liable to run into a Rou Garou on dah road.

Oh yeah!

Dat road he was famous for Rou Garous.

An ole Geebow him

he might be pour an all dat

but he gots lots of good sense.

But den

he can stay wit Margareet eeder

cause in dem days

peoples dey don sleep wit each udder until dere married.

Margareet an Geebow dey was real ole time peoples dat

believe on dah right way.

So Geebow him

he get up to leave.

He give Margareet a kiss

den he go for hees hat an he can fine it.

Dey look all over but he was gone.

Dat damn teef you know

he steal dat hat.

Ole Geebow him

he nearly have a broken heart.

Dat hat he means a lot to him.

An besides

he tink dats why Margareet he look at him dah first time.

Cause hee gots a smart hat.

An hees falcon fedder

hees Granmudder he give it to him when he was a young man

an he only wear it for very special.

Like dis night

he was very special.

Well by dah time him an dah ole lady

dey finish looking for it

he was after midnight an Geebow

he can go home cause of dah Rou Garous.

An deres no damn way Margareet hees gonna let him go eeder.

He don wan no Rou Garou to take hees man.

So

he tell him to stay

an he make him a bed on dah floor.

Boy dat teef!

He jus make it hard on dem ole peoples.

Dere was only one big room in Margareet hees house
an when dey go to bed
Margareet
he can take hees close off cause Geebow him hees
on dah floor.

An Margareet him
he don know what dat ole man he'll do if he sees
hees pettycoats.
Dat teef
he jus cause a bunch of trouble.

Well you know
when dah morning he comes
Geebow he wake up cause he hear somebody knocking on
dah door.
He never even tink
he jus jump up an he open dah door
an dere was Margareet hees granson Guspar wit dah
neighbour dere boy.
Guspar he was surprise
an kine of shame too
cause hees Granmudder he have a man in hees house.
Dats not dah kine of ting
a boy he like to tink hees Granmudder he do.

Well ole Geebow an Margareet

dey done dah bes dey could to tell dem boys what he happen

but dat neighbour boy

he go home an he tell hees Mudder what he see

an dat woman

hees got a big mout an he tell everybody.

An pretty soon

dah story of Geebow an Margareet sleeping togedder he

gets all over.

So dem ole peoples

dey gots to get married as fas as the Prees he allow dem.

An everybody

he say Margareet an Geebow dey have a shotgun wedding.

Well he wasen true.

How you can have a shotgun wedding when your over

seventy years ole?

Dats how ole dey was.

But you know what our peoples dere like.

Talking an teasing all dah time.

Ole Geebow him

he kine of like dat

cause dat kine of talk make him feel young.

But he worry bout Margareet hees repetation
cause you know
dat Margareet
he was a good Catlic woman
an he would of never have a shotgun wedding
even if he was young.

Boy dat teef
he shore cause a hell of a ruckus in dah village.
An you know
ole Geebow he never get hees hat back
but he fine hees fedder.
He was stuck on hees door frame one day when
he come home.

Some people dey say
dat dah teef
he at lees have a little respec cause he don keep
dat fedder.
But me
I know damn well why he bring it back.

Everybody in our part of dah country
knows dat Geebow him
he know Indian medicine.

Dey know too
dat fedder he was Geebows spirit.

Dat teef

he was jus damn scare when he saw what he took

dats why he bring it back.

Not because he have respec

cause dat man he never have any.

Well you know

dat teef he never change hees ways.

All hees life he steal.

He never work for a living like everybody else he do.

He have a good woman too

an a hell of a pile of kids.

Dey all turn out good dough

but dats cause hees wife he teach dem dah good way.

Hees not jus dah stealing dats bad you know.

All dough dats bad enough.

Dah real bad ting is your kids an all your granchildren.

Dey don got no good stories bout you if your a teef.

An dah stories you know

dats dah bes treasure of all to leave your family.

Everyting else on dis eart

he gets los or wore out.

But dah stories

dey las forever.

Too bad bout dat man hees kids.

Jus too bad.

Afterword

It's a great honour to be asked to share with readers, especially the educators among them, some of my thoughts on *Stories of the Road Allowance People*, and some of my experiences teaching it in university courses. I am grateful to be here and immensely happy, as many others will be, to see the revised edition of this remarkable book.

The first time I read *Stories of the Road Allowance People*, I couldn't believe my eyes and ears. Even for readers from diverse backgrounds and ethnicities, it's easy to feel the resourcefulness, warmth, and intelligence of the individuals in Maria's stories, a people both vibrant and resilient in the face of settler intrusions into their lives and lands.

When it comes to teaching this book, though, I really don't have any quick or easy solutions. Having Native background, or European or whatever, doesn't solve the challenge of teaching works outside my own specific context. And I'm aware too, from experiences both as an Aboriginal student and teacher, that the university is still a "white" space, despite positive changes, so I often feel a great unease around things like hierarchy, authority, and voice. So, the last thing I want to do when teaching *Stories of the Road Allowance People* in the classroom is get in the way of it. I'd say the same thing about many oral or written works, not just the masterpieces of Aboriginal literature.

I use the word "teach," but I think I've really been engaged in a process of trying to learn from works that I believe are important and necessary today, sharing my thoughts with others, listening to, and trying to learn from the conversations that follow. Then trying to do a better job the next time around. I know this sounds clichéd and simple, and I could pretty it up if I had to, but I think it sums up my approach.

Students are piqued by a number of questions and issues when studying *Stories of the Road Allowance People*, some of them quite challenging, so a person has to try to be ready for the discussions that will come up. For example, the use of masculine pronouns in place of feminine pronouns confuses many who haven't experienced this kind of expression. Most seem to enjoy all the "bad" English grammar and punctuation throughout, which they understand as a function of translation and voice. If we're studying another of Maria's works, say *Halfbreed*, students note the stylistic and other differences between her works. Questions about form might spark debates about the representation of Aboriginal voice in English text. A minority of students, Aboriginal and non-Aboriginal, worry that the English version might reinforce stereotypes about Native peoples. This might encourage a discussion about translation, about what gets lost or put on a backburner in the translation to English text. Students also want to know about the Road Allowance People themselves—who they were, and why they didn't legally occupy lands of their own. They enjoy the humour throughout the book, especially all the good, titillating stuff. And they're intrigued by Sherry Farrell Racette's paintings, and they wonder how these richly evocative illustrations work in conjunction with, or supplement, the stories. They also want to know about other Métis authors and artists, and about research in the area. That's a quick sample of the kinds of questions and topics that have come up.

I've been fortunate along the road to have found or stumbled on some helpful resources to help me think through some of the contexts surrounding this book. Here are a few suggested writers and subject areas, not in any order. You can look up the names and dig out the sources, and find lots more: Susan Gingell's interview with Maria on translation and the specific contexts for some of the stories. I'd suggest any interview with Maria, and anything she has produced. Even if they don't directly address *Stories of the Road Allowance People*, they'll give ideas about language, culture, healing, and the role of artists. Frank Tough's research in support of the Northwestern Saskatchewan Métis land claim is important. Because of where I live and teach, Winnipeg, and because of the historic ties of the Road Allowance People to Manitoba (see *Halfbreed*), I want students to know about the Manitoba Métis Federation's ongoing, decades-old land claim to about 1.4 million acres of land in and around Winnipeg. Brenda Macdougall's research on Métis identity formation in Northwestern Saskatchewan is also important, and Jennifer Brown's scholarship on the history of the fur trade. See also Paul Chartrand's work for political and legal backgrounds. And the historical research of Olive Patricia Dickason. In the area of Aboriginal literature and scholarship, there are so many wonderful authors and scholars on both sides of the border. For Metis (with or without the accent aigu) authors, see the body of writing, including poetry, prose, critical essays, and books, by writers such as Joanne Arnott, Joseph Boyden, Warren Cariou, Marilyn Dumont, Jo-Ann Episkenew, Kristina Fagan, Emma LaRocque, Lorraine Mayer, Duncan Mercredi, Beatrice Mosionier, Sharron Proulx-Turner, Deanna Reder, and Gregory Scofield. You'll find lots of other writers, including children's literature authors, at the Pemmican Publications website. Students will also want to learn about the work of visual artists such as Christi Belcourt, Rosalie Favell, Leanne L'Hirondelle, and, of course, Sherry Farrell Racette herself. For cultural, historical, political, and Michif language resources, see the websites of the Gabriel Dumont Institute, the Manitoba Métis Federation, the Métis National Council, and the Louis Riel Institute. Do a keyword search of "Metis" at GoodMinds.com and you'll find all kinds of materials.

There's so much good stuff I've left out, but I know you'll find what's helpful for you. Expect surprises, delights, and learning on the fly. Maybe don't rush into the academic stuff all at once. Take it slow. For fun and good energy, hear some Métis fiddlers and see the Asham Stompers on *YouTube*. Look for an event or visit a Métis community near you. Above all, your students will savour the words, emotions, and actions of the individuals in *Stories of the Road Allowance People*. What they're experiencing, I think, is some of the heart of her teachers and languages that Maria has so effectively put into English.

Paul DePasquale, Winnipeg
October 8, 2010

John (Dan) Campbell— Image courtesy Maria Campbell

John (Dan) Campbell (1917-1997) hunter, trapper, storyteller, and historian was born and raised in the Big River area of North-West Saskatchewan. Educated in the old ways of his people John knew and loved the land and it was with great pride that he shared his knowledge with young people. He believed that when all else fails it will be the land that will sustain us. The following quote taken from an interview with him depicts the kind of man he was.

"Dere's lots of moving in dah stories of our peoples. Hees a good ting dat dah ole blood hees strong cause udderwise he would be easy to forget who we are. Dats why hees important for us to know dah names of dah places where we was born and growed up cause dem names and dem stories dey keep us hooked up an from dere we can go any place and we always knowed who we are. When we gets unhooked dats when it becomes dangerous."

Adrian Hope (1903-1986) was a respected Métis activist, cowboy, poet, and educator from Alberta. He was instrumental in founding the modern Alberta Métis society and the Alberta Métis Settlements in the 1930s, and he was a founding member of Alberta Native Communications. A proud Cree speaker, he was a keeper of Métis culture. Adrian Hope spent a lifetime advocating for the rights of Métis people, and was actively involved in the process which led to the Métis being included in the Constitution.

Adrian Hope—Image courtesy Denis Wall/ DWRG Press, Used with Permission.

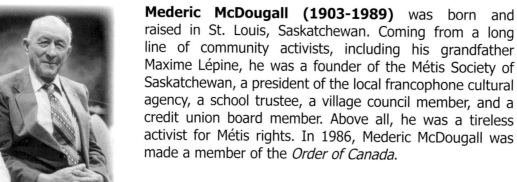

Mederic McDougall—Image courtesy, Gabriel Dumont Institute Archives, Howard and Marge Adams Collection.

Mederic McDougall (1903-1989) was born and raised in St. Louis, Saskatchewan. Coming from a long line of community activists, including his grandfather Maxime Lépine, he was a founder of the Métis Society of Saskatchewan, a president of the local francophone cultural agency, a school trustee, a village council member, and a credit union board member. Above all, he was a tireless activist for Métis rights. In 1986, Mederic McDougall was made a member of the *Order of Canada*.

Leonard Pambrun (1928-2004) was a proud Métis storyteller, horseman, and activist from Duck Lake, Saskatchewan. Instrumental in building the Métis Local and several other buildings in Duck Lake, he was also a key figure in the revival of *Back to Batoche* days in the early 1970s. He also served as president of the Duck Lake Métis Local for many years. A keeper of the Métis Oral Tradition, he shared the Old Peoples' stories with younger generations of Métis. In 1990, Leonard Pambrun was made a *Companion to the Order of Gabriel Dumont*.

Leonard Pambrun—Image courtesy Kathy Hodgson-Smith.

Maria Campbell is one of Canada's most accomplished Métis literary artists. *Halfbreed*, her poignant memoir, awakened the country to the poor social conditions facing the Métis. A highly-acclaimed writer, storyteller, playwright, and filmmaker, her broad body of work tells inspiring Métis stories with pride and compassion, with humour and sorrow, and with the same enduring spirit that keeps Métis history and culture vibrant. Through various genres of books, plays, and films, and through her ongoing work as an Elder, mentor, and community activist, Maria has made enormous contributions to both the Métis people and to Canada.

Maria Campbell—Image courtesy, Gabriel Dumont Institute Archives, Photograph by Peter Beszterda

Sherry Farrell Racette is an accomplished academic, educator, and artist whose art practice includes illustration, painting, beadwork, and textiles. She is one of the early builders of the Gabriel Dumont Institute. During her tenure with the Institute—as an educator, author, and illustrator—Sherry left an enduring legacy of highly-acclaimed resources including *The Flower Beadwork People*, *The Flags of the Métis*, and several posters, and most recently, *The Métis: A Visual History*, *Dancing in My Bones*, *Better that Way*, and *Fiddle Dancer*, which have won or have been nominated for several book awards.

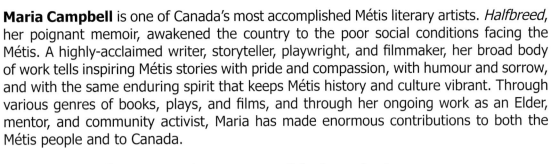

Sherry Farrell Racette— Image courtesy, Gabriel Dumont Institute Archives.

Billyjo DeLaRonde (1952-) is a lifelong Métis activist, originally from Duck Bay, Manitoba. He has held many political offices, most noticeably as President of the Manitoba Métis Federation. He takes pride in his role to replace the disrespectful statue of Louis Riel that once appeared on the grounds of the Manitoba Legislature with one more befitting Riel's stature as Manitoba's founder. He also served as the chief of the Pine Creek First Nation and as the chairperson of Frontier School Division. He is passionate about Métis people, particularly their unique and diverse heritage.

Billyjo DeLaRonde—Image courtesy, Gabriel Dumont Institute Archives, Photograph by Peter Beszterda

Roy Poitras (1939-) was born in the Lebret (Saskatchewan) Road Allowance community. He is presently an antiques dealer in Lebret. He returned to Lebret sixteen years ago after living and working in Regina. He has a great passion for Aboriginal history, and for collecting antiques and Aboriginal archival documents. A fluent Michif speaker, Roy served as the president of the Lebret Métis Local #49.

Roy Poitras—Image courtesy, Gabriel Dumont Institute Archives, Photograph by Peter Beszterda

Gilbert Anderson (1934-) comes from a large musical family and inherited a couple of family fiddles. He was always around Métis music, and continues to teach and promote fiddle and dance through the Edmonton Métis Cultural Dancers programs. He calls many of his traditional songs "Fort Edmonton" tunes.

Gilbert Anderson—Image courtesy, Gabriel Dumont Institute Archives

John Arcand (1942-) was born in 1942 near Debden, Saskatchewan. His greatest musical influences were his family, especially his father Victor and grandfather Jean-Baptiste Arcand. He currently lives near Saskatoon, Saskatchewan. He is known as the "Master of the Métis Fiddle." In 2003, John received a *National Aboriginal Achievement Award*, in 2004 he was awarded the *Saskatchewan Lieutenant Governor's Award*, and in 2007, he became a member of the *Order of Canada*.

John Arcand—Image courtesy, Gabriel Dumont Institute Archives